PERFORMANCE MANUAL

STRATEGIES
FOR TEACHING
PHYSICAL EDUCATION

CONTENTS

INTRODUCTION

Strategies for Teaching Physical Education is unique in that its major thrust divides learning experiences into teaching blocks called "teaching designs." Learning to teach in physical education must involve performance. This *Performance Manual* for *Strategies for Teaching Physical Education* contains performance evaluation forms to record competencies in which professionals should excel. Completing the required performances in this manual will not in itself make you a professional physical educator, but it is an important step toward becoming a physical education teacher.

COMPETENCY/PERFORMANCE

INSTRUCTIONS

C/P 1   When is a person physically educated? How is a physically educated person different from one who is not physically educated? It is important that physical educators construct solutions to the above questions before embarking on the journey. Before we can make plans for a trip it is imperative that we know where we are going. List those traits, attitudes, characteristics, and skills that you feel a physically educated person would possess.

C/P 2   Before setting up a physical education program for a school, there are many things that need to be considered. For example, what equipment and facilities are available in your school and community which may contribute to your physical education program? Select a secondary school that you are familiar with and list the equipment and facilities available in the school that meet the needs and interests of students in physical education. Further, list the facilities and equipment available in the community that may have physical education activity possibilities.

C/P 3   Make a list of all the physical education activities appropriate for students in your school (selected in C/P 2) which may be offered in the school and/or in the community. List these activities under the following headings: individual activities, team activities, dance activities, aquatics, self-testing activities, and recreational activities.

C/P 4   Make up course layouts for each course offered in the secondary school you selected in C/P 2. List the objectives for each course if known, the activities taught in the sequence in which they are taught, and the number of weeks spent on each activity.

1

C/P   5   Complete activity evaluation format. Follow the instructions provided on the format.

C/P   6   Out of your background and experience, formulate the major objectives of physical education. Devise a method of evaluation of activities based on your objectives to accomplish the ends illustrated in C/P 5. Evaluate physical education activities according to the evaluation format that you have devised.

C/P   7   Taking into consideration all the factors presented in C/P 1-6, make up the best required physical education program that you possibly can under conditions as they now exist (physical, administrative, facilities, etc.). For each course list the *objectives* and *units* (activities) in the *sequence* that they are to be taught and include the number of *weeks* to be spent on each unit.

C/P   8   Select a unit you expect to teach. List the specific objectives to be obtained in the unit chosen. Consider the feasibility of accomplishing these objectives within the time estimate given the unit. Incorporate the objectives into a unit introduction addressed to the students.

Outline briefly the subject matter to be used or emphasized in the unit under the following headings: history, nomenclature, terms, playing area, players, nature of the activity, rules and regulations, and safety precautions.

Select and list the pupil experiences which will insure that students will reach the desired objectives (drills, etc.). Check the proposed experiences in relationship to the objectives and subject matter outlined for the unit.

Check the total group of proposed pupil experiences and assignments in terms of consistency with the unit objectives.

List the references and materials needed for carrying out the work of the unit.

Type up the *source unit* in the form that you would want to work from.

C/P   9   For the unit selected in C/P 8, plan a day-by-day list of the learning experiences needed to meet the objectives of the unit. Write them in the sequence you plan to present them to your class.

C/P   10   What information do your students need to know about the physical education activity you selected in C/P 8—playing area, nomenclature, terms, nature of the activity, rules and regulations, safety precautions, etc.? Type the *handout* with the above information in the form that you would give to your students.

C/P   11   Construct a written test of twenty true-false items, twenty-five multiple-choice items, and one matching item with ten responses for the activity you selected in C/P 8. Type the test with instructions in the form that you would give to your students. Make an answer key for the test that you would use for grading the test.

C/P   12   Construct a skill test that will evaluate the skill of students in your class in the activity you selected in C/P 8. Type the skill test in such a manner that you could hand it to anyone in the class and they could give the test and reach the same results as you would. Include area layout-stations, equipment, scorers, recorders needed, forms for administering the test, and a description of each test item with scoring procedures.

C/P   13   In teaching activities it is important that you carefully plan your time. For the activity you selected in C/P 8, plan for a day's experiences during the unit. Fill out the Daily Time Schedule, indicating those experiences you would provide for the class with time scheduled for each activity.

C/P   14   Teachers must plan for their day's lecture if they are to be effective and not omit key points. Select a lecture that you might give to a physical education class and on the form provided type in the information you would like to have in front of you while presenting the lecture.

C/P   15   Evaluate a classmate giving a micro-lecture to the class. Fill out the evaluation form provided.

C/P   16   Present a micro-lecture of three to five minutes to the class. Give a self-evaluation of your lecture on the form provided.

C/P   17   Evaluate a classmate teaching a small group using the Introductory Design for teaching a simple skill to a small group. Fill out the Introductory Design Evaluation Form.

C/P   18   Teach a simple skill to a small group using the Introductory Design for teaching. After you have taught, fill out the self-evaluation of your teaching the Introductory Design.

C/P   19   Evaluate a classmate teaching the class by use of the Military Design. Fill out the Military Design Mini-Teaching Evaluation Form.

C/P   20   Teach a skill to the class using the Military Design. Evaluate your use of this design by filling out the Military Design Mini-Teaching Self-Evaluation Form.

C/P   21   Evaluate a classmate teaching the class by use of the Athletic Design. Fill out the Athletic Design Mini-Teaching Evaluation Form.

C/P   22   Teach a skill to the class using the Athletic Design. Evaluate your use of this design by filling out the Athletic Design Mini-Teaching Self-Evaluation Form.

C/P   23   Evaluate a classmate teaching the class by use of the Binary Design. Fill out the Binary Design Mini-Teaching Evaluation Form.

C/P   24   Teach a skill to the class using the Binary Design. Evaluate your use of this design by filling out the Binary Design Mini-Teaching Self-Evaluation Form.

C/P   25   Evaluate a classmate teaching the class by use of the Station Design. Fill out the Station Design Mini-Teaching Evaluation Form.

C/P   26   Teach a part of an activity to the class using the Station Design. Evaluate your use of this design by filling out the Station Design Mini-Teaching Self-Evaluation Form.

C/P   27   Evaluate a classmate teaching the class by use of the Team Design. Fill out the Team Design Mini-Teaching Evaluation Form.

C/P   28   Teach a part of an activity to the class using the Team Design. Evaluate your use of this design by filling out the Team Design Mini-Teaching Self-Evaluation Form.

C/P   29   Evaluate a classmate teaching the class by use of the Individual Design. Fill out the Individual Design Mini-Teaching Evaluation Form.

C/P   30   Teach a part of an activity to the class using the Individual Design. Evaluate your use of this design by filling out the Individual Design Mini-Teaching Self-Evaluation Form.

C/P   31   Evaluate a classmate teaching the class by use of the Problem Design. Fill out the Problem Design Mini-Teaching Evaluation Form.

C/P   32   Teach a part of an activity to the class using the Problem Design. Evaluate your use of this design by filling out the Problem Design Mini-Teaching Self-Evaluation Form.

C/P   33   Evaluate a classmate teaching the class by a design of his own making. Fill out the Innovative Design Mini-Teaching Evaluation Form.

C/P   34   Teach a part of an activity to the class using a design that you have devised. Evaluate your use of this design by filling out the Innovative Design Mini-Teaching Self-Evaluation Form.

C/P   35   For the activity you selected in C/P 8, plan a logical organization of experiences along the lines of one of the logical organizations for learning plans presented in class. Write out the logical organizational plan you would use in your class.

C/P   36   Select one of the readiness organizations for learning which you feel would be best to present the activity you selected in C/P 8. Describe in detail how you would implement this readiness organization in your class.

C/P   37   Evaluate a classmate teaching in the public schools. Fill out the Episode Teaching Evaluation Form provided.

C/P   38   In one of the public schools where you have been observing, teach a game or phase of an activity or skill to one of the classes (Episode Teaching). Evaluate your teaching on the evaluation form provided.

C/P   39   Review the literature in chapter 5 of *Strategies for Teaching Physical Education*. Fill out the Research Implications Form.

C/P 1
A PHYSICALLY EDUCATED PERSON

Name _____ Date _____

A physically educated person is one who demonstrates the following characteristics:

A. PHYSICAL

Values

Performance

B. SOCIAL

Values

Performance

C. EMOTIONAL

Values

Performance

D. MENTAL

Values

Performance

E. RECREATIONAL

Values

Performance

C/P 2
SCHOOL AND COMMUNITY SURVEY

Name _____ Date _____

FACILITIES IN THE SCHOOL   *FACILITIES IN THE COMMUNITY*

EQUIPMENT IN THE SCHOOL   *EQUIPMENT IN THE COMMUNITY*

Administrative procedures related to physical education in the school:

Years physical education is required ﹍﹍﹍﹍

Years physical education may be elected ﹍﹍﹍﹍

How are students assigned to physical education?

Age ﹍﹍﹍﹍

Skill ﹍﹍﹍﹍

Sex ﹍﹍﹍﹍

Other ﹍﹍﹍﹍

Are students assigned to class by grade?

Freshman ﹍﹍﹍﹍

Sophomore ﹍﹍﹍﹍

Junior ﹍﹍﹍﹍

Senior ﹍﹍﹍﹍

Other ﹍﹍﹍﹍

Explain:

C/P   3
SCHOOL ACTIVITY POTENTIAL

Name _____ Date _____

School _____

Activities that may be offered by the school and community:

INDIVIDUAL   *TEAM*

DANCE   *AQUATICS*

SELF-TESTING   *RECREATIONAL*

SCHOOL PHYSICAL EDUCATION OFFERINGS

Name _____ Date _____

PHYSICAL EDUCATION I		PHYSICAL EDUCATION II	
Unit	*No. of weeks*	*Unit*	*No. of weeks*

PHYSICAL EDUCATION III		PHYSICAL EDUCATION IV	
Unit	*No. of weeks*	*Unit*	*No. of weeks*

C/P 5
ACTIVITY EVALUATION FORMAT

Name _____ Date _____

Course Layout Format

Each activity should meet one or more of the following objectives of Physical Education:

A. Organic Power: strength, endurance, cardiovascular efficiency.

B. Neuromuscular Development: skill, grace, and efficiency of movement; skill and grace in posture; rhythm; improved reaction time; agility.

C. Personal Social Attitudes and Adjustment: self-confidence; initiative and self-direction; sociability, cooperation, friendship; leadership and ability to organize; intelligent followership; group status.

D. Interpretive and Intellectual Development: creative game strategy and techniques; knowledge and understandings of rules and etiquette; knowledge and understandings of applied anatomy, physiology and psychology; judgments in time and space.

E. Recreational Activities: after-school activity participated in for fun and satisfaction; carry-over activity for many adults.

Instructions: Below are listed activities suggested for senior high school. Rate these activities by placing the number (1) under each of the listed objectives in which that activity is below average, (2) when it is average, and (3) when that activity is above average for that objective. Place an (X) in front of all those activities your school has facilities to offer.

Activities	| *Rating in Terms of Objectives*					
individual:	A	B	C	D	E	Total
Archery	___	___	___	___	___	___
Badminton	___	___	___	___	___	___
Bait and fly cast	___	___	___	___	___	___
Bowling	___	___	___	___	___	___
Golf	___	___	___	___	___	___
Handball	___	___	___	___	___	___
Paddleball	___	___	___	___	___	___
Tennis	___	___	___	___	___	___
Track and field	___	___	___	___	___	___
Wrestling	___	___	___	___	___	___

dance:	A	B	C	D	E	Total
Acrobatic	___	___	___	___	___	_____
Folk	___	___	___	___	___	_____
Modern	___	___	___	___	___	_____
Rhythms	___	___	___	___	___	_____
Square	___	___	___	___	___	_____
Social	___	___	___	___	___	_____
Tap	___	___	___	___	___	_____

team:						
Baseball	___	___	___	___	___	_____
Basketball	___	___	___	___	___	_____
Field hockey	___	___	___	___	___	_____
Football	___	___	___	___	___	_____
Soccer	___	___	___	___	___	_____
Speedball	___	___	___	___	___	_____
Volleyball	___	___	___	___	___	_____

self-testing:						
Acrobatics	___	___	___	___	___	_____
Apparatus	___	___	___	___	___	_____
Obstacle course	___	___	___	___	___	_____
Rope-climbing	___	___	___	___	___	_____
Stunts	___	___	___	___	___	_____
Trampoline	___	___	___	___	___	_____
Tumbling	___	___	___	___	___	_____

	A	B	C	D	E	Total
formal and gymnastics:						
Body mechanics	___	___	___	___	___	___
Calisthenics	___	___	___	___	___	___
Gymnastics	___	___	___	___	___	___
Marching	___	___	___	___	___	___
aquatics:						
Swimming	___	___	___	___	___	___
Synchronized swimming	___	___	___	___	___	___
Water polo	___	___	___	___	___	___
Water safety	___	___	___	___	___	___
recreational:						
Hockey	___	___	___	___	___	___
Camping	___	___	___	___	___	___
Card games	___	___	___	___	___	___
Checkers	___	___	___	___	___	___
Chess	___	___	___	___	___	___
Croquet	___	___	___	___	___	___
Dart ball	___	___	___	___	___	___
Duckpins	___	___	___	___	___	___
Hiking	___	___	___	___	___	___
Shuffleboard	___	___	___	___	___	___

ACTIVITY EVALUATION

Name _____ Date _____

School _____

Objectives

A.

B.

C.

D.

E.

Method of Evaluation:

Activities   *Rating in Terms of Objectives*

	A	B	C	D	E	Total
_____	____	____	____	____	____	_____
_____	____	____	____	____	____	_____
_____	____	____	____	____	____	_____
_____	____	____	____	____	____	_____
_____	____	____	____	____	____	_____
_____	____	____	____	____	____	_____
_____	____	____	____	____	____	_____
_____	____	____	____	____	____	_____
_____	____	____	____	____	____	_____
_____	____	____	____	____	____	_____
_____	____	____	____	____	____	_____
_____	____	____	____	____	____	_____

16

Activities   *Rating in Terms of Objectives*

	A	B	C	D	E	Total
_____	___	___	___	___	___	___
_____	___	___	___	___	___	___
_____	___	___	___	___	___	___
_____	___	___	___	___	___	___
_____	___	___	___	___	___	___
_____	___	___	___	___	___	___
_____	___	___	___	___	___	___
_____	___	___	___	___	___	___
_____	___	___	___	___	___	___
_____	___	___	___	___	___	___
_____	___	___	___	___	___	___
_____	___	___	___	___	___	___
_____	___	___	___	___	___	___
_____	___	___	___	___	___	___
_____	___	___	___	___	___	___
_____	___	___	___	___	___	___
_____	___	___	___	___	___	___
_____	___	___	___	___	___	___
_____	___	___	___	___	___	___
_____	___	___	___	___	___	___
_____	___	___	___	___	___	___
_____	___	___	___	___	___	___
_____	___	___	___	___	___	___

COURSE LAYOUTS

Name _____ Date _____

PHYSICAL EDUCATION I

Objectives:

Unit   No. of weeks

_____

Total

PHYSICAL EDUCATION II

Objectives:

Unit   No. of weeks

_____

Total

PHYSICAL EDUCATION III

Objectives:

Unit   No. of weeks

                        _____

                           Total

PHYSICAL EDUCATION IV

Objectives:

Unit   No. of weeks

                                                  —————————
                                                  Total

SOURCE UNIT

Name _____ Date _____

Title _____

HISTORY:

NOMENCLATURE:

TERMS:

22

PLAYING AREA:

PLAYERS:

NATURE OF ACTIVITY:

RULES AND REGULATIONS:

SAFETY PRECAUTIONS:

SKILLS AND TEACHING POINTS:

24

INDIVIDUAL DRILLS:

GROUP DRILLS:

COMBINATION DRILLS AND LEAD-UP GAMES:

UNIT LAYOUT

Name _____ Date _____

Month _____ Year _____ Unit Title _____

Monday	Tuesday	Wednesday	Thursday	Friday

Name _____ Date _____

Month _____ Year _____ Unit Title _____

Monday	Tuesday	Wednesday	Thursday	Friday

Name _____ Date _____

Unit Title _____

NOMENCLATURE:

TERMS:

NATURE OF GAME:

RULES AND REGULATIONS:

WRITTEN TEST

Name _____ Date _____

Unit Test in _____

Section 1. *True-False Items*

Instructions: If the statement is true, circle the letter T beside the number of the statement; if the statement is false or partially false, circle the letter F beside the number of the statement. Each correct answer will count 1 point.

T   F   1.

Section 2. *Multiple-Choice Items*

Instructions: Choose the answer that completes the sentence or is the best answer for the beginning phrase. Place the letter of that response in the corresponding blank. Each correct answer will count 2 points.

————————   1.

Section 3. *Matching Items*

Instructions: Match the definitions in the left-hand column with the proper term in the right-hand column. Place the identifying letter of the proper term in the blank space provided. Each correct answer will count 3 points.

———————   1.

SKILL TEST

Name _____ Date _____

Skill Test in _____

Area Layout—Stations

Equipment, Scorers, Recorders Needed

Forms for Administering Skill Test

TASK 1

Description:

Scoring:

TASK 2

Description:

Scoring:

TASK 3

Description:

Scoring:

TASK 4

Description:

Scoring:

TASK 5

Description:

Scoring:

DAILY TIME SCHEDULE

Name _____ Date _____

Grade _____ Unit _____ Lesson _____

OBJECTIVES:

AREA LAYOUT:

EQUIPMENT AND MATERIALS:

TIME SCHEDULE:

PRACTICE—DRILLS:

TEACHING POINTS:

C/P 14
DAILY LESSON PLAN (Lecture)

Name _____ Date _____

Title _____

OBJECTIVES:

AUDIO-VISUAL AIDS:

REFERENCES:

INTRODUCTION:

PRESENTATION (EXPLANATION–OUTLINE):

DEMONSTRATION:

APPLICATION:

SUMMARY:

ASSIGNMENT:

C/P   15
MICRO-LECTURE EVALUATION

Name _____ Date _____

Micro-Teacher _____ Lecture Title _____

	Yes	No	?
INTRODUCTION			
1. Students can see and hear			
2. Student warm-up			
3. Relates to previous knowledge			
4. Enthusiasm—motivation			
5. Defines terms			
DIRECT COMMUNICATION			
1. Correct pronouncement of words			
2. Talks to everyone			
3. Faces and talks to class			
4. Repeats main points			
5. Knows subject			
6. Employs humor			
7. Interest in subject			
8. Cheerful			
9. Enthusiastic			
10. Showmanship—use of audio-visual aids			
INDIRECT COMMUNICATION			
1. Stands in position for attention			
2. Meaningful gestures			
3. Judges effectiveness (observes expressions)			
4. Confidence in ability			
5. Stimulates discussion			
6. Changes pace of speaking			
7. Informal methods of presentation			
8. Holds respect of class			
9. Interacts with class			

	Yes	No	?
VOICE			
1. Speaks loudly enough without shouting			
2. Tone of voice friendly			
3. Speaks with enthusiasm			
4. Speaks clearly			
5. Makes point clear			
6. Uses voice to give emphasis			
DISTRACTIONS			
1. Abusive language			
2. Sarcasm			
3. Personal mannerisms			
4. Talks to blackboard or wall			
5. Habitual gestures			
6. Temper			
7. Negative teaching			
8. Discipline			
9. Word repetition			
10. Impatient			
11. Answered own question			
12. Loss of sequence			
13. Class confusion			

ADDITIONAL COMMENTS:

Did micro-teacher meet objectives of the lesson? Explain.

C/P 16
MICRO-LECTURE SELF-EVALUATION

Name _____ Date _____

Lecture Title _____

	Yes	No	?
INTRODUCTION			
1. Students can see and hear			
2. Student warm-up			
3. Relates to previous knowledge			
4. Enthusiasm—motivation			
5. Defines terms			
DIRECT COMMUNICATION			
1. Correct pronouncement of words			
2. Talks to everyone			
3. Faces and talks to class			
4. Repeats main points			
5. Knows subject			
6. Employs humor			
7. Interest in subject			
8. Cheerful			
9. Enthusiastic			
10. Showmanship—use of audio-visual aids			
INDIRECT COMMUNICATION			
1. Stands in position for attention			
2. Meaningful gestures			
3. Judges effectiveness (observes expressions)			
4. Confidence in ability			
5. Stimulates discussion			
6. Changes pace of speaking			
7. Informal methods of presentation			
8. Holds respect of class			
9. Interacts with class			

	Yes	No	?
VOICE			
1. Speaks loudly enough without shouting			
2. Tone of voice friendly			
3. Speaks with enthusiasm			
4. Speaks clearly			
5. Makes point clear			
6. Uses voice to give emphasis			
DISTRACTIONS			
1. Abusive language			
2. Sarcasm			
3. Personal mannerisms			
4. Talks to blackboard or wall			
5. Habitual gestures			
6. Temper			
7. Negative teaching			
8. Discipline			
9. Word repetition			
10. Impatient			
11. Answered own question			
12. Loss of sequence			
13. Class confusion			

How well did I accomplish what I set out to accomplish?

INTRODUCTORY DESIGN MICRO-TEACHING EVALUATION

Name _____ Date _____

Micro-Teacher _____ Skill Taught _____

Procedure	NA	0	1	2	3
PHASE I INTRODUCTION					
1. Students can see and hear					
2. Student warm-up					
3. Relates to previous knowledge					
4. Logical sequence					
5. Enthusiasm—motivation					
PHASE II TEACHER INSTRUCTS AND DEMONSTRATES					
1. Teaching points (one fundamental)					
2. Emphasis on teaching points					
3. Relates to previous learning					
4. Demonstration					
5. Order of presentation					
6. Repetition of key points					
PHASE III STUDENTS TELL, TEACHER DOES					
1. Each student tells (what to do, how to do it)					
2. Teacher asks good questions					
a. Clear, brief, challenging					
b. Directed to class as a whole					
c. Calls on specific student					
d. Insists on individual response					
3. Evaluates answers and emphasizes correct response					
4. Students' knowledge of procedure					
PHASE IV STUDENTS TELL AND DO					
1. Each student does activity					
2. Teacher stresses correct action					
3. Teacher praises when warranted					
4. If student forgets, teacher:					
a. Stops him					
b. Asks challenging questions					

*NA—Not Applicable; 0—Left out; 1—Poor; 2—Average; 3—Very good

	NA	0	1	2	3

PHASE V   PRACTICE

	NA	0	1	2	3
1. Selects drill for individual help					
2. Teacher gives good drill instructions					
3. Emphasizes accuracy of movement					
4. Insists on procedure taught					
5. Reteaches when necessary					

MANAGEMENT

	NA	0	1	2	3
1. Room conditions (heat, light, etc.)					
2. Equipment and facilities availability					
3. Class arrangement (sun, wind, crowding, etc.)					
4. Placement of equipment					
5. Use of equipment (minimum disturbance)					

GENERAL CONDUCT OF LESSON

	NA	0	1	2	3
1. Voice					
a. Loud enough					
b. Friendly tone					
c. Enthusiasm					
d. Speaks clearly					
2. Talks to class					
3. Eye contact					
4. Judges effect (students' expressions, etc.)					
5. Teacher has neat appearance					
6. Teacher controls temper					
7. Teacher is cheerful					
8. Teacher has good posture					
9. Student interest					
10. Student participation					
11. Teacher's knowledge of subject					
12. Use of techniques					
13. Use of methods					

DISTRACTIONS

Type	Mark	Describe
1. Negative teaching		
2. Distracting mannerism		
3. Discipline		
4. Word repetition		
5. Sarcasm		
6. Habitual gestures		
7. Impatient		
8. Additional instr. (phases III and IV)		
9. Takes activity from student		
10. Dwells on mistakes		
11. Answers own questions		
12. Loss of sequence		
13. Class confusion		

Did micro-teacher accomplish what he set out to accomplish?

INTRODUCTORY DESIGN MICRO-TEACHING SELF-EVALUATION

Name _____ Date _____

_____ Skill Taught _____

Procedure	*Evaluation*				
	NA	0	1	2	3
PHASE I INTRODUCTION					
1. Students can see and hear					
2. Student warm-up					
3. Relates to previous knowledge					
4. Logical sequence					
5. Enthusiasm—motivation					
PHASE II TEACHER INSTRUCTS AND DEMONSTRATES					
1. Teaching points (one fundamental)					
2. Emphasis on teaching points					
3. Related to previous learning					
4. Demonstration					
5. Order of presentation					
6. Repetition of key points					
PHASE III STUDENTS TELL, TEACHER DOES					
1. Each student tells (what to do, how to do it)					
2. Teacher asks good questions					
a. Clear, brief, challenging					
b. Directed to class as a whole					
c. Calls on specific student					
d. Insists on individual response					
3. Evaluates answers and emphasizes correct response					
4. Students' knowledge of procedure					
PHASE IV STUDENTS TELL AND DO					
1. Each student does activity					
2. Teacher stresses correct action					
3. Teacher praises when warranted					
4. If student forgets, teacher:					
a. Stops him					
b. Asks challenging questions					

	NA	0	1	2	3

PHASE V PRACTICE

	NA	0	1	2	3
1. Selects drill for individual help					
2. Teacher gives good drill instructions					
3. Emphasizes accuracy of movement					
4. Insists on procedure taught					
5. Reteaches when necessary					

MANAGEMENT

	NA	0	1	2	3
1. Room conditions (heat, light, etc.)					
2. Equipment and facilities availability					
3. Class arrangement (sun, wind, crowding, etc.)					
4. Placement of equipment					
5. Use of equipment (minimum disturbance)					

GENERAL CONDUCT OF LESSON

	NA	0	1	2	3
1. Voice					
a. Loud enough					
b. Friendly tone					
c. Enthusiasm					
d. Speaks clearly					
2. Talks to class					
3. Eye contact					
4. Judges effect (students' expressions, etc.)					
5. Teacher has neat appearance					
6. Teacher controls temper					
7. Teacher is cheerful					
8. Teacher has good posture					
9. Student interest					
10. Student participation					
11. Teacher's knowledge of subject					
12. Use of techniques					
13. Use of methods					

DISTRACTIONS

Type	Mark	Describe
1. Negative teaching		
2. Distracting mannerism		
3. Discipline		
4. Word repetition		
5. Sarcasm		
6. Habitual gestures		
7. Impatient		
8. Additional instr. (phases III and IV)		
9. Takes activity from student		
10. Dwells on mistakes		
11. Answers own questions		
12. Loss of sequence		
13. Class confusion		

How well did I accomplish what I set out to accomplish?

C/P 19

MILITARY DESIGN MINI-TEACHING EVALUATION

Name ______________________ Date __________

Evaluator No. 2 ______________________

Mini-Teacher ______________ Skill Taught __________

Procedure	*Evaluation* NA	0	1	2	3
PHASE I INTRODUCTION					
1. Equipment in formation					
2. Students line up by equipment					
3. Facilities (lighting, heating, etc.)					
4. Use of area					
5. Motivation					
6. Relates to previous knowledge					
PHASE II INSTRUCTION–DEMONSTRATION					
1. Demonstrates at standard speed					
2. Demonstrates using different view					
3. Points out key points					
4. Order of presentation					
5. Demonstration effectiveness					
PHASE III IMITATION					
1. Students pick up equipment					
2. Teacher (or skilled student) faces away from class					
3. Teacher (or skilled student) performs, pointing out each step					
4. Students imitate movement of teacher					
5. Repeats several times					
6. Teacher relates each step to number					
7. Teacher calls numbers in skill rhythm					
8. Repeats several times					
9. Continues performance until students grasp movement					
PHASE IV PERFORMANCE					
1. Assigns student to call numbers					
2. Removes image					
3. Student calls numbers in rhythm					
4. Teacher observes each student					
5. Teacher stops and reteaches incorrect performance					
6. Continues until some degree of uniformity					

	NA	0	1	2	3

PHASE V   INDIVIDUAL DRILL

	NA	0	1	2	3
1. Selects drill for individual help					
2. Instructions for drill					
3. Emphasizes accuracy of movement					
4. Insists on procedure taught					
5. Reteaches when necessary					
6. Teacher in position to teach individual student					
7. Students handle all equipment					

PHASE VI   TEAM DRILL

	NA	0	1	2	3
1. Selects drill for optimum participation					
2. Instructions					
3. Observes all students					
4. Optimum use of equipment and facilities					
5. Continues to teach where needed					
6. Emphasizes accuracy and speed of movement					
7. Students handle all equipment					

PHASE VII   SUMMARY

	NA	0	1	2	3
1. Demonstration					
2. Teaching points					
3. Discussion					

MANAGEMENT

	NA	0	1	2	3
1. Room conditions (heat, light, etc.)					
2. Equipment and facilities availability					
3. Class arrangement (sun, wind, crowding, etc.)					
4. Placement of equipment					
5. Use of equipment (minimum disturbance)					

GENERAL CONDUCT OF LESSON

	NA	0	1	2	3
1. Voice					
a. Loud enough					
b. Friendly tone					
c. Enthusiasm					
d. Speaks clearly					
2. Talks to class					
3. Eye contact					

	NA	0	1	2	3

GENERAL CONDUCT OF LESSON (Continued)

	NA	0	1	2	3
4. Judges effect (students' expressions, etc.)					
5. Teacher has neat appearance					
6. Teacher controls temper					
7. Teacher is cheerful					
8. Teacher has good posture					
9. Student interest					
10. Student participation					
11. Teacher's knowledge of subject					
12. Use of techniques					

DISTRACTIONS

Type	Mark	Describe
1. Negative teaching		
2. Distracting activity		
3. Discipline		
4. Word repetition		
5. Sarcasm		
6. Habitual gestures		
7. Impatient		
8. Additional instr. (phases III and IV)		
9. Takes activity from student		
10. Handles equipment		
11. Use of area		
12. Loss of sequence		
13. Class confusion		
14. Sun, lighting, etc.		

How well did mini-teacher achieve stated objectives?

MILITARY DESIGN MINI-TEACHING SELF-EVALUATION

Name _____ Date _____

Evaluator No. 2 _____

_____ Skill Taught _____

Procedure	NA	0	1	2	3
PHASE I INTRODUCTION					
1. Equipment in formation					
2. Students line up by equipment					
3. Facilities (lighting, heating, etc.)					
4. Use of area					
5. Motivation					
6. Relates to previous knowledge					
PHASE II INSTRUCTION–DEMONSTRATION					
1. Demonstrates at standard speed					
2. Demonstrates using different view					
3. Points out key points					
4. Order of presentation					
5. Demonstration effectiveness					
PHASE III IMITATION					
1. Students pick up equipment					
2. Teacher (or skilled student) faces away from class					
3. Teacher (or skilled student) performs, pointing out each step					
4. Students imitate movement of teacher					
5. Repeats several times					
6. Teacher relates each step to number					
7. Teacher calls numbers in skill rhythm					
8. Repeats several times					
9. Continues performance until students grasp movement					
PHASE IV PERFORMANCE					
1. Assigns student to call numbers					
2. Removes image					
3. Student calls numbers in rhythm					
4. Teacher observes each student					
5. Teacher stops and reteaches incorrect performance					
6. Continues until some degree of uniformity					

	NA	0	1	2	3
PHASE V INDIVIDUAL DRILL					
1. Selects drill for individual help					
2. Instructions for drill					
3. Emphasizes accuracy of movement					
4. Insists on procedure taught					
5. Reteaches when necessary					
6. Teacher in position to teach individual student					
7. Students handle all equipment					
PHASE VI TEAM DRILL					
1. Selects drill for optimum participation					
2. Instructions					
3. Observes all students					
4. Optimum use of equipment and facilities					
5. Continues to teach where needed					
6. Emphasizes accuracy and speed of movement					
7. Students handle all equipment					
PHASE VII SUMMARY					
1. Demonstration					
2. Teaching points					
3. Discussion					
MANAGEMENT					
1. Room conditions (heat, light, etc.)					
2. Equipment and facilities availability					
3. Class arrangement (sun, wind, crowding, etc.)					
4. Placement of equipment					
5. Use of equipment (minimum disturbance)					
GENERAL CONDUCT OF LESSON					
1. Voice					
a. Loud enough					
b. Friendly tone					
c. Enthusiasm					
d. Speaks clearly					
2. Talks to class					
3. Eye contact					

	NA	0	1	2	3

GENERAL CONDUCT OF LESSON (Continued)

	NA	0	1	2	3
4. Judges effect (students' expressions, etc.)					
5. Teacher has neat appearance					
6. Teacher controls temper					
7. Teacher is cheerful					
8. Teacher has good posture					
9. Student interest					
10. Student participation					
11. Teacher's knowledge of subject					
12. Use of techniques					

DISTRACTIONS

Type	Mark	Describe
1. Negative teaching		
2. Distracting activity		
3. Discipline		
4. Word repetition		
5. Sarcasm		
6. Habitual gestures		
7. Impatient		
8. Additional instr. (phases III and IV)		
9. Takes activity from student		
10. Handles equipment		
11. Use of area		
12. Loss of sequence		
13. Class confusion		
14. Sun, lighting, etc.		

How well did I achieve stated objectives?

C/P 21
ATHLETIC DESIGN MINI-TEACHING EVALUATION

Name _____ Date _____

Evaluator No. 2 _____

Mini-Teacher _____ Skill Taught _____

Procedure	*Evaluation*				
	NA	0	1	2	3
PHASE I INTRODUCTION					
1. Can students see and hear					
2. Relates to previous knowledge					
3. Logical sequence					
4. Enthusiasm—motivation					
PHASE II DEMONSTRATION—INSTRUCTION					
1. Performs activity at operating speed					
2. Performs activity again, slowly pointing out key points					
3. Teaching points (one fundamental)					
4. Related to previous learning					
5. Demonstration—instruction effectiveness					
6. Repetition of key points					
PHASE III REPETITION OF PERFORMANCE					
1. Repeats performance, slightly slower than operating speed					
2. Shows class different view					
3. Restates procedure					
4. Asks questions of class					
PHASE IV STUDENT DEMONSTRATION					
1. Calls on student to demonstrate					
2. Student demonstrates					
3. Student points out key points					
4. Question and answer period					
PHASE V INDIVIDUAL DRILL					
1. Selects drill for individual help					
2. Instructions for drill					
3. Emphasizes accuracy of movement					
4. Insists on procedure taught					
5. Reteaches when necessary					
6. Teacher in position to teach individual student					
7. Students handle all equipment					

	NA	0	1	2	3
PHASE VI TEAM DRILL					
1. Selects drill for optimum participation					
2. Instructions					
3. Observes all students					
4. Optimum use of equipment and facilities					
5. Continues to teach where needed					
6. Emphasizes accuracy and speed of movement					
7. Students handle all equipment					
8. Utilizes area					
PHASE VII SUMMARY					
1. Demonstration					
2. Teaching points					
3. Discussion					
MANAGEMENT					
1. Room conditions (heat, light, etc.)					
2. Equipment and facilities availability					
3. Class arrangement (sun, wind, crowding, etc.)					
4. Placement of equipment					
5. Use of equipment (minimum disturbance)					
GENERAL CONDUCT OF LESSON					
1. Voice					
a. Loud enough					
b. Friendly tone					
c. Enthusiasm					
d. Speaks clearly					
2. Talks to class					
3. Eye contact					
4. Judges effect (students' expressions, etc.)					
5. Teacher has neat appearance					
6. Teacher controls temper					
7. Teacher is cheerful					
8. Teacher has good posture					
9. Student interest					
10. Student participation					

	NA	0	1	2	3
GENERAL CONDUCT OF LESSON (Continued)					
11. Teacher's knowledge of subject					
12. Use of techniques					

DISTRACTIONS

Type	Mark	Describe
1. Negative teaching		
2. Distracting activity		
3. Discipline		
4. Word repetition		
5. Sarcasm		
6. Habitual gestures		
7. Impatient		
8. Additional instr. (phases III and IV)		
9. Takes activity from student		
10. Handles equipment		
11. Answers own questions		
12. Loss of sequence		
13. Class confusion		

How well did mini-teacher achieve stated objectives?

ATHLETIC DESIGN MINI-TEACHING SELF-EVALUATION

Name _____ Date _____

Evaluator No. 2 _____

_____ Skill Taught _____

Procedure	*Evaluation*				
	NA	0	1	2	3
PHASE I INTRODUCTION					
1. Students see and hear					
2. Relates to previous knowledge					
3. Logical sequence					
4. Enthusiasm—motivation					
PHASE II DEMONSTRATION—INSTRUCTION					
1. Performs activity at operating speed					
2. Performs activity again, slowly pointing out key points					
3. Teaching points (one fundamental)					
4. Relates to previous learning					
5. Demonstration—instruction effectiveness					
6. Repetition of key points					
PHASE III REPETITION OF PERFORMANCE					
1. Repeats performance, slightly slower than operating speed					
2. Shows class different view					
3. Restates procedure					
4. Asks questions of class					
PHASE IV STUDENT DEMONSTRATION					
1. Calls on student to demonstrate					
2. Student demonstrates					
3. Student points out key points					
4. Question and answer period					
PHASE V INDIVIDUAL DRILL					
1. Selects drill for individual help					
2. Instructions for drill					
3. Emphasizes accuracy of movement					
4. Insists on procedure taught					
5. Reteaches when necessary					
6. Teacher in position to teach individual student					
7. Students handle all equipment					

	NA	0	1	2	3

PHASE VI   TEAM DRILL

	NA	0	1	2	3
1. Selects drill for optimum participation					
2. Instructions					
3. Observes all students					
4. Optimum use of equipment and facilities					
5. Continues to teach where needed					
6. Emphasizes accuracy and speed of movement					
7. Students handle all equipment					
8. Utilizes area					

PHASE VII   SUMMARY

	NA	0	1	2	3
1. Demonstration					
2. Teaching points					
3. Discussion					

MANAGEMENT

	NA	0	1	2	3
1. Room conditions (heat, light, etc.)					
2. Equipment and facilities availability					
3. Class arrangement (sun, wind, crowding, etc.)					
4. Placement of equipment					
5. Use of equipment (minimum disturbance)					

GENERAL CONDUCT OF LESSON

	NA	0	1	2	3
1. Voice					
a. Loud enough					
b. Friendly tone					
c. Enthusiasm					
d. Speaks clearly					
2. Talks to class					
3. Eye contact					
4. Judges effect (students' expressions, etc.)					
5. Teacher has neat appearance					
6. Teacher controls temper					
7. Teacher is cheerful					
8. Teacher has good posture					
9. Student interest					

	NA	0	1	2	3

GENERAL CONDUCT OF LESSON (Continued)

	NA	0	1	2	3
10. Student participation					
11. Teacher's knowledge of subject					
12. Use of techniques					

DISTRACTIONS

Type	Mark	Describe
1. Negative teaching		
2. Distracting activity		
3. Discipline		
4. Word repetition		
5. Sarcasm		
6. Habitual gestures		
7. Impatient		
8. Additional instr. (phases III and IV)		
9. Takes activity from student		
10. Handles equipment		
11. Answers own questions		
12. Loss of sequence		
13. Class confusion		

How well did I achieve stated objectives?

C/P 23
BINARY DESIGN MINI-TEACHING EVALUATION

Name _____ Date _____

Evaluator No. 2 _____

Mini-Teacher _____ Skill Taught _____

Procedure	*Evaluation*				
	NA	0	1	2	3
PHASE I INTRODUCTION					
1. Facilities (lighting, heating, etc.)					
2. Students paired					
3. Each pair assigned station					
4. Equipment assigned to each pair					
5. Enthusiasm—motivation					
6. All can see and hear					
PHASE II INSTRUCTION–DEMONSTRATION					
1. Demonstrates at standard speed					
2. Demonstrates—points out key points at each step					
3. Explains each step of procedure					
4. Repeats instruction					
5. Asks good questions					
6. Requires complete answers					
PHASE III SET A PERFORMS, SET B TELLS					
1. Assigns Set A equipment					
2. Set A performs skill					
3. Set B observes					
4. Set B checks performance					
5. Set B reminds partner of steps of procedure					
6. Instructor observes each pair					
7. Reinstructs when necessary					
PHASE IV SET B PERFORMS, SET A TELLS					
1. Assigns Set B equipment					
2. Set B performs skill					
3. Set A observes					
4. Set A checks B's performance					
5. Set A reminds B of steps of procedure					
6. Instructor observes each pair					
7. Reinstructs when necessary					

	NA	0	1	2	3
PHASE V INDIVIDUAL DRILL					
1. Selects drill for individual help					
2. Instructions for drill					
3. Emphasizes accuracy of movement					
4. Insists on procedure taught					
5. Reteaches when necessary					
6. Teacher in position to teach individual student					
7. Students handle all equipment					
PHASE VI TEAM DRILL					
1. Selects drill for optimum participation					
2. Instructions					
3. Observes all students					
4. Optimum use of equipment and facilities					
5. Continues to teach where needed					
6. Emphasizes accuracy and speed of movement					
7. Students handle all equipment					
PHASE VII SUMMARY					
1. Demonstration					
2. Teaching points					
3. Discussion					
MANAGEMENT					
1. Room conditions (heat, light, etc.)					
2. Equipment and facilities availability					
3. Class arrangement (sun, wind, crowding, etc.)					
4. Placement of equipment					
5. Use of equipment (minimum disturbance)					
GENERAL CONDUCT OF LESSON					
1. Voice					
a. Loud enough					
b. Friendly tone					
c. Enthusiasm					
d. Speaks clearly					

	NA	0	1	2	3

GENERAL CONDUCT OF LESSON (Continued)

	NA	0	1	2	3
2. Talks to class					
3. Eye contact					
4. Judges effect (students' expressions, etc.)					
5. Teacher has neat appearance					
6. Teacher controls temper					
7. Teacher is cheerful					
8. Teacher has good posture					
9. Student interest					
10. Student participation					
11. Teacher's knowledge of subject					
12. Use of techniques					

DISTRACTIONS

Type	Mark	Describe
1. Negative teaching		
2. Distracting activity		
3. Discipline		
4. Word repetition		
5. Sarcasm		
6. Habitual gestures		
7. Impatient		
8. Additional instr. (phases III and IV)		
9. Takes activity from student		
10. Handles equipment		
11. Answers own questions		
12. Loss of sequence		
13. Class confusion		

Did mini-teacher achieve stated objectives?

BINARY DESIGN MINI-TEACHING SELF-EVALUATION

Name _____ Date _____

Evaluator No. 2 _____

_____ Skill Taught _____

Procedure	*Evaluation*				
	NA	0	1	2	3
PHASE I INTRODUCTION					
1. Facilities (lighting, heating, etc.)					
2. Students paired					
3. Each pair assigned station					
4. Equipment assigned to each pair					
5. Enthusiasm—motivation					
6. All can see and hear					
PHASE II INSTRUCTION—DEMONSTRATION					
1. Demonstrates at standard speed					
2. Demonstrates—points out key points at each step					
3. Explains each step of procedure					
4. Repeats instruction					
5. Asks good questions					
6. Requires complete answers					
PHASE III SET A PERFORMS, SET B TELLS					
1. Assigns Set A equipment					
2. Set A performs skill					
3. Set B observes					
4. Set B checks performance					
5. Set B reminds partner of steps of procedure					
6. Instructor observes each pair					
7. Reinstructs when necessary					
PHASE IV SET B PERFORMS, SET A TELLS					
1. Assigns Set B equipment					
2. Set B performs skill					
3. Set A observes					
4. Set A checks B's performance					
5. Set A reminds B of steps of procedure					
6. Instructor observes each pair					
7. Reinstructs when necessary					

	NA	0	1	2	3

PHASE V   INDIVIDUAL DRILL

	NA	0	1	2	3
1. Selects drill for individual help					
2. Instructions for drill					
3. Emphasizes accuracy of movement					
4. Insists on procedure taught					
5. Reteaches when necessary					
6. Teacher in position to teach individual student					
7. Students handle all equipment					

PHASE VI   TEAM DRILL

	NA	0	1	2	3
1. Selects drill for optimum participation					
2. Instructions					
3. Observes all students					
4. Optimum use of equipment and facilities					
5. Continues to teach where needed					
6. Emphasizes accuracy and speed of movement					
7. Students handle all equipment					

PHASE VII   SUMMARY

	NA	0	1	2	3
1. Demonstration					
2. Teaching points					
3. Discussion					

MANAGEMENT

	NA	0	1	2	3
1. Room conditions (heat, light, etc.)					
2. Equipment and facilities availability					
3. Class arrangement (sun, wind, crowding, etc.)					
4. Placement of equipment					
5. Use of equipment (minimum disturbance)					

GENERAL CONDUCT OF LESSON

	NA	0	1	2	3
1. Voice					
a. Loud enough					
b. Friendly tone					
c. Enthusiasm					
d. Speaks clearly					

	NA	0	1	2	3

GENERAL CONDUCT OF LESSON (Continued)

	NA	0	1	2	3
2. Talks to class					
3. Eye contact					
4. Judges effect (students' expressions, etc.)					
5. Teacher has neat appearance					
6. Teacher controls temper					
7. Teacher is cheerful					
8. Teacher has good posture					
9. Student interest					
10. Student participation					
11. Teacher's knowledge of subject					
12. Use of techniques					

DISTRACTIONS

Type	Mark	Describe
1. Negative teaching		
2. Distracting activity		
3. Discipline		
4. Word repetition		
5. Sarcasm		
6. Habitual gestures		
7. Impatient		
8. Additional instr. (phases III and IV)		
9. Takes activity from student		
10. Handles equipment		
11. Answers own questions		
12. Loss of sequence		
13. Class confusion		

Did I achieve stated objectives?

C/P   25
STATION DESIGN MINI-TEACHING EVALUATION

Name _____ Date _____

Evaluator No. 2 _____

Mini-Teacher _____

Activity _____ Skill Taught _____

STATION ORGANIZATION:	COMMENTS:
INTRODUCTION:	
INSTRUCTION–DEMONSTRATION:	
PRACTICE:	
SUMMARY:	

Strong Points:

Weak Points:

STATION DESIGN MINI-TEACHING SELF-EVALUATION

Name _____ Date _____

Activity _____ Skill Taught _____

STATION ORGANIZATION:	*COMMENTS:*
INTRODUCTION:	
INSTRUCTION–DEMONSTRATION:	
PRACTICE:	
SUMMARY:	

Strong Points:

Weak Points:

C/P 27
TEAM DESIGN MINI-TEACHING EVALUATION

Name _____ Date _____

Evaluator No. 2 _____

Activity _____ Skill Taught _____

INTRODUCTION:	*COMMENTS:*
INSTRUCTION–DEMONSTRATION:	
DESIGN IMPLEMENTATION:	
PRACTICE:	
SUMMARY:	

Strong Points:

Weak Points:

TEAM DESIGN MINI-TEACHING SELF-EVALUATION

Name _____ Date _____

Activity _____ Skill Taught _____

INTRODUCTION:	COMMENTS:
INSTRUCTION–DEMONSTRATION:	
DESIGN IMPLEMENTATION:	
PRACTICE:	
SUMMARY:	

Strong Points:

Weak Points:

C/P 29
INDIVIDUAL DESIGN MINI-TEACHING EVALUATION

Name _____ Date _____

Evaluator No. 2 _____

Activity _____ Skill Taught _____

INTRODUCTION: *COMMENTS:*

HANDOUT:

INSTRUCTIONS:

PRACTICE:

SUMMARY:

Strong Points:

Weak Points:

INDIVIDUAL DESIGN MINI-TEACHING SELF-EVALUATION

Name _____ Date _____

Activity _____ Skill Taught _____

INTRODUCTION:	COMMENTS:
HANDOUT:	
INSTRUCTIONS:	
PRACTICE:	
SUMMARY:	

Strong Points:

Weak Points:

C/P 31
PROBLEM DESIGN MINI-TEACHING EVALUATION

Name _____ Date _____

Evaluator No. 2 _____

Activity _____ Skill Taught _____

INTRODUCTION: *COMMENTS:*

DESIGN:

PRACTICE:

SUMMARY:

Strong Points:

Weak Points:

PROBLEM DESIGN MINI-TEACHING SELF-EVALUATION

Name _____ Date _____

Activity _____ Skill Taught _____

INTRODUCTION:	COMMENTS:
DESIGN:	
PRACTICE:	
SUMMARY:	

Strong Points:

Weak Points:

INNOVATIVE DESIGN MINI-TEACHING EVALUATION

Name _____ Date _____

Evaluator No. 2 _____

Activity _____ Skill Taught _____

INTRODUCTION:

COMMENTS:

DESIGN:

PRACTICE:

SUMMARY:

Strong Points:

Weak Points:

INNOVATIVE DESIGN MINI-TEACHING SELF-EVALUATION

Name _____ Date _____

Activity _____ Skill Taught _____

INTRODUCTION: | *COMMENTS:*

DESIGN:

PRACTICE:

SUMMARY:

Strong Points:

Weak Points:

C/P 35
LOGICAL ORGANIZATION FOR LEARNING

Name _____ Date _____

Month _____ Year _____ Unit _____

Monday	Tuesday	Wednesday	Thursday	Friday

Name _____ Date _____

Month _____ Year _____ Unit _____

Monday	Tuesday	Wednesday	Thursday	Friday

C/P 36
READINESS ORGANIZATION FOR LEARNING

Name _____ Date _____

Month _____ Year _____ Unit _____

Description

Plan

Monday	Tuesday	Wednesday	Thursday	Friday

C/P 37
EPISODE TEACHING EVALUATION

Cooperating Teacher _____

Name _____ Date _____

It is not intended that the following areas of teacher competence will have equal weight in evaluation, nor are they listed in order of importance. On the line opposite major headings place an X under the appropriate term. The X can be placed anywhere on the continuum. For minor headings place Xs under the evaluation continuum to give an idea of how major heading evaluation was derived.

PERSONAL QUALITIES

	Poor	Accept-able	Good	Out-standing

CLASSROOM PERSONALITY

Sense of humor?
Poise?
Cheerfulness?
Temper control?
Punctual?
Patience?

PERSONAL APPEARANCE

Neat and clean?
Annoying mannerisms?
Tasteful dress?

SOCIAL

Cooperates with teachers?
Tactful?
Tolerant of other teachers?
Respect for slow learners?
Enjoys teaching?

HEALTH

Good posture?
Good physical fitness?
Good health?
Extra energy?

	Poor	Accept- able	Good	Out- standing

VOICE AND SPEECH

    Pleasing voice?
    Good modulation?
    Forceful?
    Correct pronunciation?

USE OF LANGUAGE

    Large vocabulary?
    Clearly presents ideas?
    Speaks well outside class?
    Ability to simplify?

CREATIVITY

    Initiative?
    Resourcefulness?
    Enthusiasm?
    New ideas and methods?
    Leadership?

PROFESSIONAL COMPETENCY

COMMAND OF SUBJECT MATTER

    Broad understanding in and outside area?
    Knows special content area?
    Skill in correlating subject matter?
    Philosophy well defined?

ABILITY TO ORGANIZE AND PLAN

    Are teaching objectives written?
    Are teaching objectives clear?
    Are plans adequate?
    Are plans prepared in advance?
    Reports in on time?

	Poor	Accept-able	Good	Out-standing

. *CLASSROOM MANAGEMENT AND DISCIPLINE*

Good class control?
Good discipline?
Good use of time?
Give individual help?

USE OF RESOURCES

Are students motivated?
Are audio-visual materials used?
Are current events used?
Are community resources used?

TEACHING ABILITY

Uses principles of learning?
Positive help to students?
Helps students adjust?
Uses teaching progression?
Involves students?
Provides for individual differences?

EVIDENCE OF PROFESSIONAL GROWTH

Reacts to criticism or suggestions?
Takes part in school activities?
Professional meetings?
Self-improvement, reading, etc.?

Overall estimation of strengths and
weaknesses which may affect student
teacher's success in teaching. Please
list specific comments below:

Evaluator _____

School _____ Subject _____

Grade Level _____ Probable Grade _____

EPISODE TEACHING SELF-EVALUATION

Name _____ Date _____

It is not intended that the following areas of teacher competence will have equal weight in evaluation, nor are they listed in order of importance. On the line opposite major headings place an X under the appropriate term. The X can be placed anywhere on the continuum. For minor headings place Xs under the evaluation continuum to give an idea of how major heading evaluation was derived.

PERSONAL QUALITIES

	Poor	Accept-able	Good	Out-standing

CLASSROOM PERSONALITY

    Sense of humor?

    Poise?

    Cheerfulness?

    Temper control?

    Punctual?

    Patience?

PERSONAL APPEARANCE

    Neat and clean?

    Annoying mannerisms?

    Tasteful dress?

SOCIAL

    Cooperate with teachers?

    Tactful?

    Tolerant of other teachers?

    Respect for slow learners?

    Enjoy teaching?

HEALTH

    Good posture?

    Good physical fitness?

    Good health?

    Extra energy?

	Poor	Accept-able	Good	Out-standing

VOICE AND SPEECH

    Pleasing voice?

    Good modulation?

    Forceful?

    Correct pronunciation?

USE OF LANGUAGE

    Large vocabulary?

    Clearly present ideas?

    Speak well outside class?

    Ability to simplify?

CREATIVITY

    Initiative?

    Resourcefulness?

    Enthusiasm?

    New ideas and methods?

    Leadership?

PROFESSIONAL COMPETENCY

COMMAND OF SUBJECT MATTER

    Broad understanding in and outside
        your area?

    Know your special content area?

    Skill in correlating subject matter?

    Philosophy well defined?

ABILITY TO ORGANIZE AND PLAN

    Are teaching objectives written?

    Are teaching objectives clear?

    Are plans adequate?

    Are plans prepared in advance?

    Reports in on time?

	Poor	Accept-able	Good	Out-standing

CLASSROOM MANAGEMENT AND DISCIPLINE

    Good class control?

    Good discipline?

    Good use of time?

    Give individual help?

USE OF RESOURCES

    Are students motivated?

    Are audio-visual materials used?

    Are current events used?

    Are community resources used?

TEACHING ABILITY

    Use principles of learning?

    Positive help to students?

    Help students adjust?

    Use teaching progression?

    Involve students?

    Provide for individual differences?

EVIDENCE OF PROFESSIONAL GROWTH

    React to criticism or suggestions?

    Take part in school activities?

    Professional meetings?

    Self-improvement, reading, etc.?

    Overall estimation of strengths and weaknesses which may affect your success in teaching. Please list specific comments below:

School _____ Subject _____

Grade Level _____ Probable Grade _____

C/P   39
RESEARCH IMPLICATIONS

Name _____ Date _____

TECHNIQUES

Ref. No.	Activity	Comparison	Results

METHODS

Ref. No.	Activity	Comparison	Results

DESIGN

Ref. No.	Activity	Comparison	Results

ORGANIZATION FOR LEARNING

Ref. No.	Activity	Comparison	Results

C/P   39
RESEARCH IMPLICATIONS (Continued)

REFERENCES

1.

2.

3.

4.

5.

6.

7.

8.

9.

10.

11.

12.

13.

14.

15.

16.

17.

18.

19.

20.

21.

22.

23.

24.

25.

26.

27.

28.

29.

30.

31.

32.

33.

34.

35.

36.

37.

38.

39.

40.

41.

42.

43.

DAILY TIME SCHEDULE

Name _____ Date _____

Activity _____ Skill _____

OBJECTIVES:	AREA LAYOUT:
EQUIPMENT AND MATERIALS:	
TIME SCHEDULE:	PRACTICE–DRILLS:

TEACHING POINTS:

DAILY TIME SCHEDULE

Name _____ Date _____

Activity _____ Skill _____

OBJECTIVES:	*AREA LAYOUT:*
EQUIPMENT AND MATERIALS:	
TIME SCHEDULE:	*PRACTICE–DRILLS:*

TEACHING POINTS:

DAILY TIME SCHEDULE

Name _____ Date _____

Activity _____ Skill _____

OBJECTIVES:

AREA LAYOUT:

EQUIPMENT AND MATERIALS:

TIME SCHEDULE:

PRACTICE–DRILLS:

TEACHING POINTS:

DAILY TIME SCHEDULE

Name _____ Date _____

Activity _____ Skill _____

OBJECTIVES:	*AREA LAYOUT:*
EQUIPMENT AND MATERIALS:	
TIME SCHEDULE:	*PRACTICE–DRILLS:*

TEACHING POINTS:

DAILY TIME SCHEDULE

Name _____ Date _____

Activity _____ Skill _____

OBJECTIVES:	AREA LAYOUT:
EQUIPMENT AND MATERIALS:	
TIME SCHEDULE:	PRACTICE–DRILLS:

TEACHING POINTS:

DAILY TIME SCHEDULE

Name _____ Date _____

Activity _____ Skill _____

OBJECTIVES:

AREA LAYOUT:

EQUIPMENT AND MATERIALS:

TIME SCHEDULE:

PRACTICE–DRILLS:

TEACHING POINTS:

DAILY TIME SCHEDULE

Name _____ Date _____

Activity _____ Skill _____

OBJECTIVES:	*AREA LAYOUT:*
EQUIPMENT AND MATERIALS:	
TIME SCHEDULE:	*PRACTICE–DRILLS:*

TEACHING POINTS:

DAILY TIME SCHEDULE

Name _____ Date _____

Activity _____ Skill _____

OBJECTIVES:

AREA LAYOUT:

EQUIPMENT AND MATERIALS:

TIME SCHEDULE:

PRACTICE–DRILLS:

TEACHING POINTS:

DAILY TIME SCHEDULE

Name _____ Date _____

Activity _____ Skill _____

OBJECTIVES:

AREA LAYOUT:

EQUIPMENT AND MATERIALS:

TIME SCHEDULE:

PRACTICE–DRILLS:

TEACHING POINTS:

DAILY TIME SCHEDULE

Name _____ Date _____

Activity _____ Skill _____

OBJECTIVES:

AREA LAYOUT:

EQUIPMENT AND MATERIALS:

TIME SCHEDULE:

PRACTICE—DRILLS:

TEACHING POINTS:

UNIT LAYOUT

Name _____ Date _____

Month _____ Year _____ Unit _____

Monday	Tuesday	Wednesday	Thursday	Friday

UNIT LAYOUT

Name _____ Date _____

Month _____ Year _____ Unit _____

Monday	Tuesday	Wednesday	Thursday	Friday

UNIT LAYOUT

Name _____ Date _____

Month _____ Year _____ Unit _____

Monday	Tuesday	Wednesday	Thursday	Friday

UNIT LAYOUT

Name _____ Date _____

Month _____ Year _____ Unit _____

Monday	*Tuesday*	*Wednesday*	*Thursday*	*Friday*

UNIT LAYOUT

Name _____ Date _____

Month _____ Year _____ Unit _____

Monday	Tuesday	Wednesday	Thursday	Friday

UNIT LAYOUT

Name _____ Date _____

Month _____ Year _____   Unit _____

Monday	Tuesday	Wednesday	Thursday	Friday

UNIT LAYOUT

Name _____ Date _____

Month _____ Year _____   Unit _____

Monday	Tuesday	Wednesday	Thursday	Friday

UNIT LAYOUT

Name _____ Date _____

Month _____ Year _____ Unit _____

Monday	Tuesday	Wednesday	Thursday	Friday

UNIT LAYOUT

Name _____ Date _____

Month _____ Year _____ Unit _____

Monday	Tuesday	Wednesday	Thursday	Friday